AF885177
15⁵⁰
art
#294

Gay Games III Vancouver, Canada
Celebration `90

THE WOMEN

Photography by
Cheryl A. Traendly

Acknowledgments

I would like to thank the following people for their help, suggestions and support in creating this book with me:

Anita Kennedy

Susan Minde

Barbara Tobin and Cass Smith

Cora Smith Tobin, age seven months (special supervisor)

Gina Nellor and Marilyn Chuck of the Printing Depot

Caren Callahan

Joan Bobkoff for her fine photography

All the participants and athletes who responded to my questionnaire and shared their feelings and experiences with me. Many of their quotes may be found throughout the book.

Disclaimer Statement

These photographs were taken in Vancouver, Canada, between August 4–12, 1990. All events were photographed as part of *Gay Games III – Celebration '90.* This was an event for Gays and Lesbians to celebrate who they are - some with friends and relatives. Some of the volunteers, spectators and participants are not of the Gay/Lesbian Community. Please do not make an assumption about the sexuality of anyone who appears in this book.

Views expressed on the back cover are the opinions of the individual listed, not necessarily that of the publication and /or organization.

First Edition
© 1992 by Cheryl A. Traendly Productions
All rights are reserved. No part of this book may be reproduced or utilized in any way or by any means including, but not limited to, electronic or mechanical, without permission in writing from the publisher. Inquiries may be addressed to:

Cheryl A. Traendly Productions
P.O. Box 68
Eldridge, CA 95431-0068

Library of Congress Catalog Card # 92–93515

ISBN # 0–9634389–9–9

Cover Design: Cheryl Traendly and Valerie McDowell

Typesetting: Valerie McDowell, Desktop Designs Unlimited

Printing: Odell Printing

Contents

Foreword by Cheryl A. Traendly

When I made my reservations for Gay Games III, I already knew I would publish a book featuring the women. It was a tremendous commitment and challenge - exciting and frightening. Thinking about it made me feel anxious and overwhelmed.

Women in sports are often poorly portrayed visually and for years I have tried to expand the image of women athletes by capturing their emotion and attitude during different aspects of their lives; at home, during training, in triumph and disappointment, in frustration and at peace.

As a sports photographer for the past fifteen years, I have often felt frustrated with how my images were used. Once the photos or slides were sent to a magazine or book publisher, I had no input as to how a photo was cropped, sized or positioned on a page. I felt my photographic abilities were compromised, and I felt like screaming when an art editor cropped off the legs of an athlete in action, or cut off the head or hands to conveniently fit into a column.

Getting an assignment, photographing and seeing a few photos published was never very satisfying. Something was missing. The process was incomplete. I decided to photograph an event, produce a book and control every step through completion.

I chose to photograph Gay Games III because, as a lesbian, I wanted to chronicle the event showing the women - who they are, how they got there, why they participated, and what they experienced.

This is my vision of Gay Games III, showing the preparation, action, friendship and fun.

I gave it my best shot. Enjoy!

Opening Ceremonies

"The experience of the Games is everlasting. If I ever again have that feeling of being the only one, I only need to think about the Opening Ceremony. It was such an incredible, empowering experience. The Games demonstrated that we are truly everywhere and everyone."

Pat McGarvey

The athletes of our world. They came to Vancouver...

Photo by Joan Bobkoff

"Opening Ceremonies were a real high for me – to see so many proud, strong people together – celebrating."

Kathryn Running

Photo by Joan Bobkoff

"The Opening Ceremonies were awesome. It was exhilarating to feel the warmth and love of so many people. To look up and see thousands of family and friends applauding us ... to know it was at last OK to be me."

Sarah Davis

Photo by Joan Bobkoff

We Marched.

We Laughed.

We Sang.

We Felt Proud!

ALBANY
TEAM NY
CELEBRATES
THE LESBIAN
GAY 90's!
GAY GAMES III
VANCOUVER B.C.
WE REMEMBER.

The parade continues as 7500 athletes enter B.C. Place Stadium

"These Games represented the most dynamic world-wide movement for social change based on a simple dream ... the right to love!"

Robin Tyler

Photo by Joan Bobkoff

Celebration '90 Festival Chorus was organized and conducted by Carol White

FESTIVAL CHORUS

Celebration
'90
Festival Chorus

Photo by Joan Bobkoff

Let the Games begin!

Croquet

Jean Hernandez – Seattle, WA – lines up shot

Jean Hernandez (left) and Danette Leon Hardin (right)

Marathon

Marathon, Racewalk, Physically Challenged 10K

7:00 am – The start in Stanley Park

Jorge Alvarez and Alicia Hays lead the way

126

442

Running the marathon was special for many athletes. It was an international competition without pressure, allowing each to run at her own pace.

Feeling light — breathing easy. What a glorious day!

Showing their best form are a few of the 750 athletes from the San Francisco Bay Area

417

Finishing together ...

... has its rewards

"One more loop ..."

Char Levitt, running for the Virgin Islands, was the second woman to finish in the Marathon

Only 8 miles to go!

One of the many volunteers who reached out to the lesbian and gay community

The family of Darold Slack show their love and support

"At long last I reached the sound tunnel of people leading to the finish line. The drama of the moment overwhelmed me. I started crying the last 50 meter 'sprint' to the finish ... my final time was 3 hours, 5 minutes."

Debbie Chaddock

Martial Arts

Linda Ransom – Black Belt weapons champion

Sensei Linda Ramzy is a certified 2nd Degree Black Belt in the Fuji Ryu Ju-Jitsu system of self defense. Her proficiency and versatility in the martial arts has earned her many honors as a finalist and first place winner at various tournaments around the country. She is presently employed as the Chief Instructor and Consultant for Self Defense and Rape Prevention at Princeton University and Dartmouth University.

Judges flash their score as 400 spectators enjoy a Kata performance

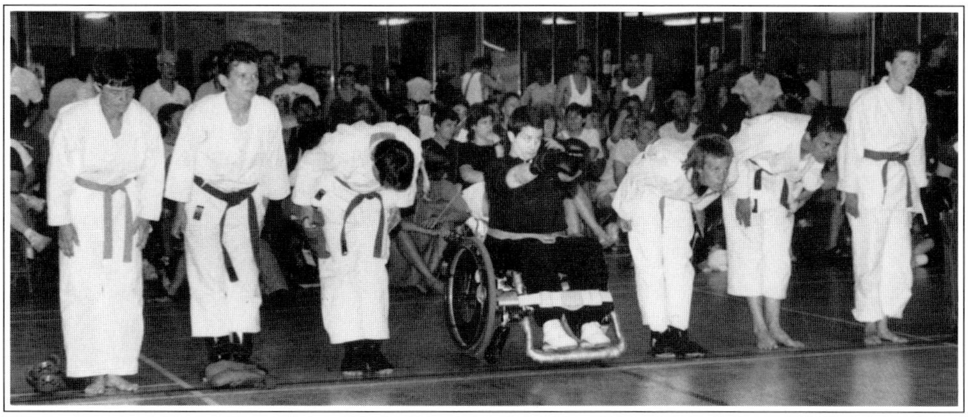

Photo by Joan Bobkoff

Kate Cloudparks, an inspiration on wheels

Photo by Joan Bobkoff

TAEKWON DO
SEATTLE WA.

"I felt a great sense of comradeship. It was wonderful to meet people from all over North America and Europe, from many different styles, not only Japanese karate but kung fu, tae kwon do, judo, aikido, etc. The other wonderful thing was seeing so many women black belts together in one place. In traditional competitions, there are fewer women black belts. In this one, there were more women than men, of high caliber, and enough women to form a masters division (over 35 years old) – unheard of by me in regular competition."

Sarah Payne,
Vancouver, B.C.

Physique

Opening march – Orpheum Theater

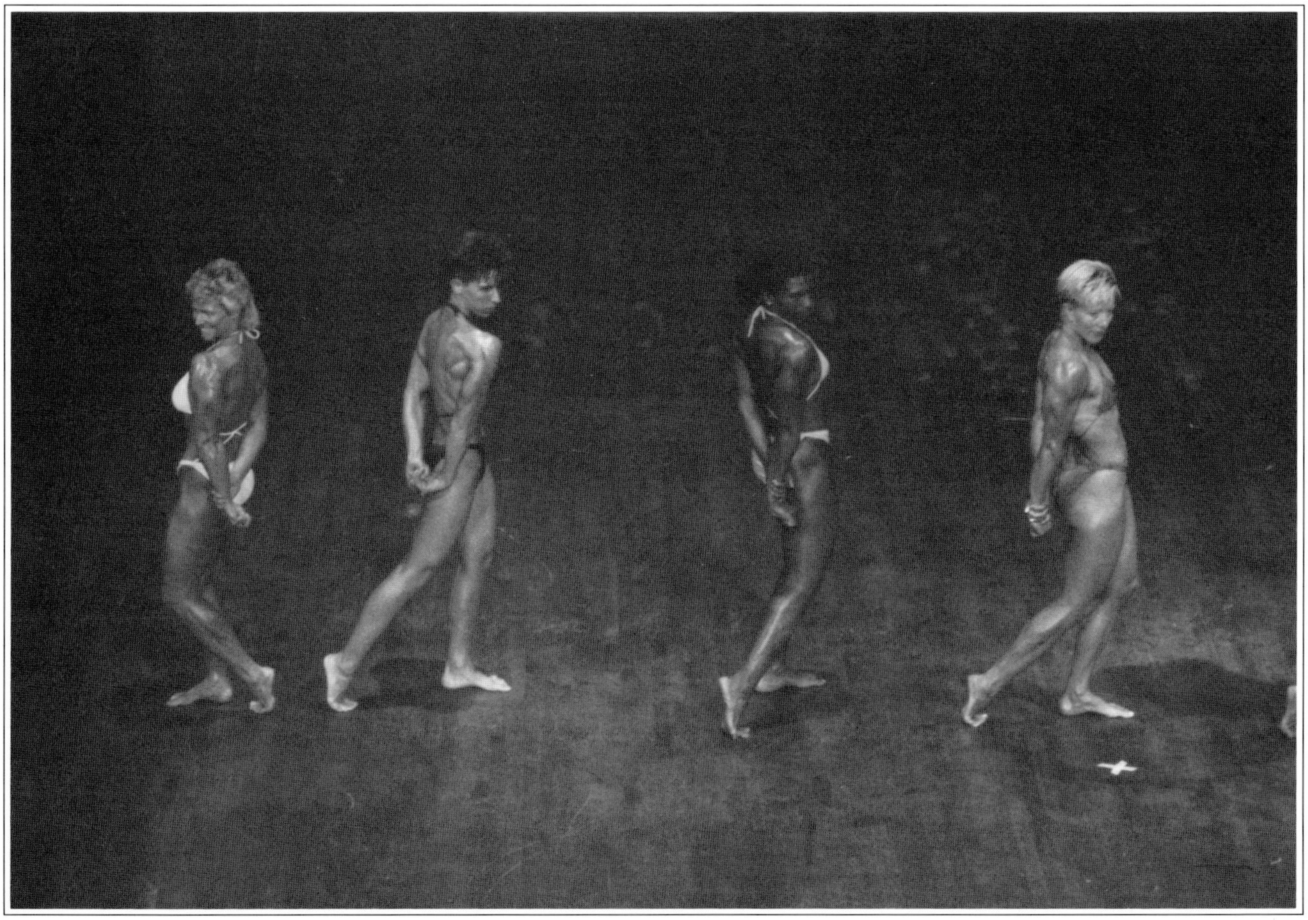

Heavyweight contestants strut their stuff

Janet Wingett –
gold medal winner, heavyweight

Liz White, best poser

Lightweight winner Rosemary Comthe

Lightweight class contestants

Gail Winston – over 50 gold medal winner

Preparation – Susan Minde applies oil to Caren Callahan while Maddy Hirschfield looks on

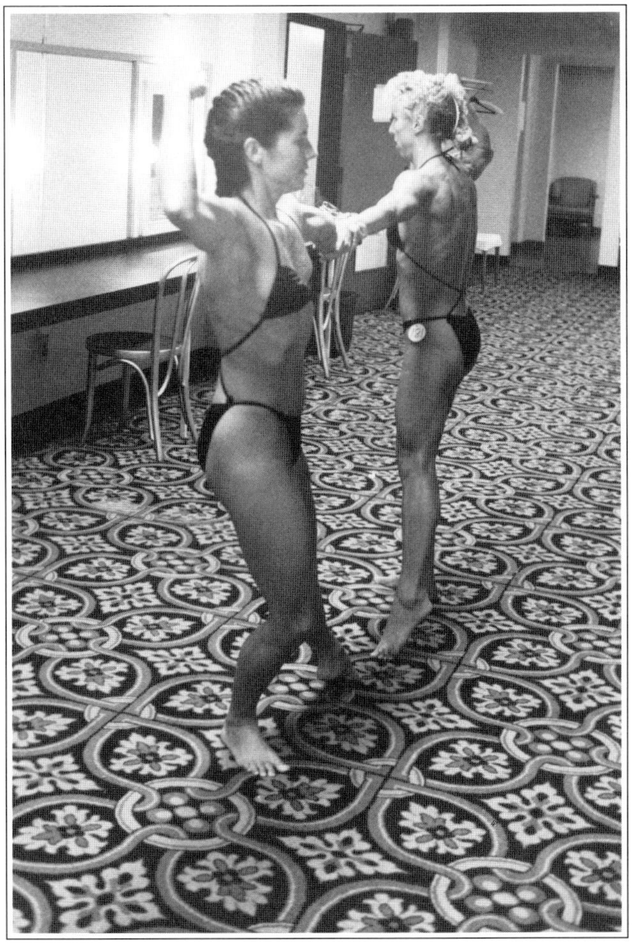

Practice ...

Pride!

B.C. Cliver (left) and Kitty Tsui (right), pairs gold medal winners

Joanna Lynn, heavyweight

Middleweights Diane Aaronson (left), Cynthia Ann Sherman (center) and Shelly Alexander (right)

Powerlifting

Concentration

The Squat

The Return

Support and caring were evident for these athletes to give their personal best.

Soccer

Pursuit ... at Strathcona Park

Relaxing between matches

The pass ...

The kick ...

The save ...

Softball

Coach of the Ballbusters from N.Y.

Out at first.

Not a shadow of a doubt ...

Doesn't everyone wear Birkenstocks ...?

Swimming

DSST

DSST

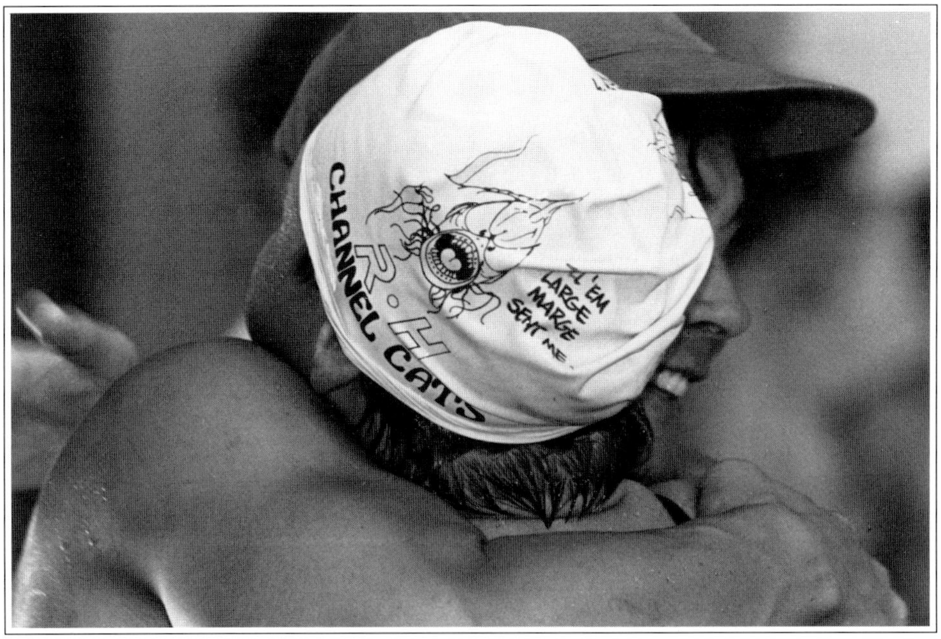
CHANNEL CATS
R. H
LARGE
MARGE
SENT ME

"As a participant in Gay Games III, I experienced growth in my openness about being a lesbian in the public eye and it continues to grow today."

Amy Stewart

Start of race at the beautiful Vancouver Aquatic Center's 50 metre indoor pool where over 600 swimmers participated

Sarah Davis (age 66)

"I decided to participate in the Games because of my love for swimming, and my age. I felt that since I'd not competed before, I'd better hurry – at 66 years old. My life is affected by having an increase in my health – better endurance and strength, better cardio-vascular system, better definition and an increase in self-esteem. Probably another significant result of the Games for me was completely and irrevocably coming out of the closet and being highly visible as a lesbian and a winner. I've also become aware of how much more there always is to learn. I'm motivated to continue the 'Personal Best' efforts – improving my stroke style as well as times in swimming events. Although I've been a 'good' swimmer all of my life, I'm aware of how much more I can refine my efforts. It's fun, it's healthy and I love it. It's so rewarding to accomplish the next minor goal, be it an arm swing, a kick or hand position. And the comraderie is another bene."

Sarah Davis

B.J. Miller congratulates her partner Sarah Davis

Tennis

On the courts at Jericho Park

Track & Field

"I had the desire to compete in Track and Field with other lesbians. I haven't yet come across any other athletic-minded dykes in Australia and it was wonderful to be amongst hundreds of 'em in Vancouver."

Annette Shiels

Photo by Joan Bobkoff

Annette Shiels from Australia

"I loved the cheers that the older and the less-successful athletes received. The spirit of participation and non-judgmental attitudes were excellent. I also enjoyed all the amazing variations — sizes, color, shapes, etc. of women that attended. It's nice to know that lesbians come from all over, and are different and similar ..."

Niamh Walsh

Niamh Walsh from Ireland, winner of 4 gold medals

"Benefits for me from G.G. III included a desire to return to running, coming out at home due to fundraising efforts, and a great joy and pride in being a lesbian. For the next Games, I want to organize an Irish team so that many more could enjoy and find pride in the event."

Niamh Walsh

Another benefit of the Games was to exchange team pins, flags, and addresses.

Mary Taylor, daughter:

"My reasons for participating in the Games changed over time. At first, I wanted to compete in track and field. My goal was to 'simply' win a medal. After a few months of training, my enthusiasm grew. I wanted to share this experience with my family so I asked my mother to run with me. My mother, now 54, once ran competitively. I wanted her to have a chance to run again. We spent the next year training together. Through this time, I began to sense a broader purpose to the Games than just competing and winning. I saw the Games as an opportunity for our community to stand together and unite."

Glenna Taylor, mother:

"In August of 1989, my daughter Mary invited me to participate with her in the track events of the Gay Games. I was very excited and touched by her invitation to be part of her celebration. We trained together for a full year and the experience brought us closer together with even greater love and understanding of each other. Even before we left for Vancouver, Mary's young friends were so supportive of me, and their encouragement will always be a sweet memory for me. The loving companionship that I witnessed throughout the Games will stay with me always. As I think back to watching the track events, the roar of the crowd was as great for the first runners across the finish line as for the courageous efforts of the last runners. Each runner seemed to be greeted at the finish line by a hug and words of praise for their efforts, which at times made me reflect on the fact of whether the result would have been the same in my straight world."

"Through sports, I have found that I can easily establish a common bond with women of all cutures. I want to be around those women who are pushing their bodies to the limit because I want to press my body as hard as I can."

Vivien Herrera

COLORADO

Triathlon

Triathlon Photos by Joan Bobkoff

BODY

176

235

Volleyball

Photo by Joan Bobkoff

"I wanted to play volleyball with international teams. I needed to be around 'family' and feel the energy."

Cici Cole

CHICAGO
11
CHICAGO
10
13
23

5

Teams & Groups

We Were There!

Hawaiian slow pitch team

TEAM
PORTLAND

7
51
11
10
13
10
3

Amsterdam Team – Volleyball

Racewalker winners

Other Favorites

Vancouver as viewed from the Croquet Field, Jericho Park

Our team spirit was enchanced by the beauty of our surroundings.

Closing Ceremonies, with athletes from 30 countries, taking home memories of fun, competition and friendship

Entertainer at Opening Ceremonies

Casade Cloggers

Photo by Joan Bobkoff

Cultural Festival's Dancelebration!